Music and Dra
CIRCLE TIME

Quick, easy ideas for active participation

Written and compiled by CAROL GNOJEWSKI ✦ Illustrated by BARB TOURTILLOTTE

Totline® Publications

A Division of Frank Schaffer Publications, Inc.
Torrance, California

Totline Publications would like to thank the following people for their contributions to this book: Barbara Backer, Charleston, SC; Betty Ruth Baker, Waco, TX; Gayle Bittinger, Marysville, WA; Janice Bodenstedt, Jackson, MI; Marie Cecchini, Hughsonville, NY; Ann-Marie Donovan, Framingham, MA; Adele Engelbracht, River Ridge, LA; Wes Epperson, Placerville, CA; Karen Folk, Franklin, MA; Deborah Garmon, Groton, CT; Allyson Goldberg, Elkton, MD; Margo Hunter, Westerville, OH; Sister Linda Kaman, RSM, Pittsburgh, PA; Dr. Margery Kranyik, Hyde Park, MA; Kathy McCullough, St. Charles, IL; Judith McNitt, Adrian, MI; Diana Nazaruk, Clark Lake, MI; Susan M. Paprocki, Northbrook, IL; Susan Peters, Upland, CA; Andy Plumb, Greenbrae, CA; Lois E. Putnam, Pilot Mountain, NC; Beverly Qualheim, Manitowoc, WI; Janet Reeves, Livermore Falls, ME; Sara R. Salzberg, Brighton, MA; Betty Silkunas, North Wales, PA; Shana Sloan, Everett, WA; Heather Tekavec, Langley, BC; Diane Thom, Maple Valley, WA; Steven and Susan Traugh, Idyllwild, CA.

Managing Editor: Kathleen Cubley
Contributing Editors: Susan Hodges, Elizabeth McKinnon, Durby Peterson, Susan M. Sexton, Jean Warren
Copyeditor: Kris Fulsaas
Proofreader: Miriam Bulmer
Editorial Assistant: Durby Peterson
Graphic Designer (Interior): Sarah Ness
Layout Artists: Sarah Ness, Laura Horman
Graphic Designer (Cover): Brenda Mann Harrison
Production Manager: Melody Olney

ISBN: 1-57029-240-X

Library of Congress Catalog Card Number 98-61458
Printed in the United States of America
Published by Totline® Publications
23740 Hawthorne Blvd.
Torrance, CA 90505

20 19 18 17 16 15 14 13 12 11 10 9 8 7 6 5 4 3 2

Introduction

Music and Dramatics at Circle Time is designed as a reference book for preschool teachers, offering easy, engaging activities for turning circle time into learning time.

The activities in this book introduce young children to the concepts of music, movement, and dramatic play. Because young children like to be actively involved, these activities engage the children in many ways. The focus of some activities is to encourage listening, watching, and imitating. The focus of other activities is to work together as a group or with a partner to solve problems. In still others, the children are encouraged to create and sustain a pretend play environment.

Music and Dramatics at Circle Time was conceived as a resource for group activities. These activities help to build trust and community through shared experience. However, personal creativity and expression are also valued. Often, the children will be invited to relate a personal experience or to lead the group in a game or movement.

Language is another key component of all of the activities, and group discussion emerges as an important part of the circle time experience. But oral communication is not the only type of communication emphasized in this book. Music and body language are also introduced as ways to express and share ideas, stories, and feelings.

There is really no right or wrong group size for circle time activities. It all depends on your children, the help you have, and what you are comfortable with. Since movement is involved, make sure there is adequate space in your circle time area for the children to run, stretch, jump, and twirl around without bumping into anyone or anything. Taking circle time outside for these activities is also an option.

Music, movement, and dramatic play help to foster both the imagination and physical and mental fitness. They are essential ingredients in a well-rounded curriculum. It is our hope that these activities will help preschool teachers find new and engaging ways to incorporate these concepts into their day.

Contents

Music and Instruments

Music and Movement

Dramatic Play

Music and Instruments

Music Everywhere

Help your children understand that musical sounds can come from many different sources. In the middle of your circle, set out a variety of everyday items that make sounds, including wind chimes, doorbells, kitchen timers, radios, music boxes, squeeze toys, watches, and wind-up toys. Let your children play with and listen to the items. Ask them questions about each item: "Where might you find it? Have you heard this sound before? What other items around the room can make musical sounds?"

Nature Sounds

Bring in relaxation tapes for your children to listen to. Many of these tapes mix soft music with soothing natural sounds such as rain falling, waves breaking, birds singing, wind blowing, and crickets or frogs chirping. Have the children try to identify each natural sound. Talk about how hearing these sounds can remind you of a specific memory or place, such as playing at the beach or hiking in the forest.

Music Detectives

Have your children sit in a circle in the middle of the room with their eyes closed. (Provide them with stocking caps to pull over their eyes as blindfolds to keep them from peeking, if you wish.) Move around the circle humming or singing a simple tune. Invite the children to listen carefully and try to figure out where they think the music is coming from. Stay in one spot and have the children point to where they think the music is; then have them open their eyes (or remove their blindfolds). Did they guess correctly? Let the children take turns being the Music Detectives and the singer.

Musical Echoes

Invite your children to form a circle, with you in the middle. Make sure that all of the children are facing you. Then pick a simple, general theme, such as fruits, animals, flowers, or toys. Chant "I like _____," and complete the sentence with a specific example of the theme you have chosen, such as "I like peaches," or "I like dogs." Have the children repeat your sentence back to you. Give each child a turn in the middle.

Variations:

- Have each child build upon your sentence, so "I like peaches" becomes "I like peaches and plums" and then "I like peaches, plums, and cherries."

- Clap or stamp out the rhythm as you chant.

- Echo the rhythm of each sentence using rhythm instruments instead of words.

- Echo the rhythm of each sentence using *la, ti,* or other do-re-mi solmization syllables instead of words.

Music Match

Record the sounds of various rhythm instruments. Then place these instruments in the middle of your circle. As you play the recording for your children, have them take turns experimenting with the instruments to discover which made each sound.

Variation: Record pieces of music that feature a variety of other solo instruments, including brass, percussion, wind, and string instruments. Set out pictures of each instrument and let the children guess which picture matches which sound.

Listening for Parts and Wholes

Invite each of your children to choose one instrument from a variety of classroom rhythm instruments placed in your circle, including rhythm sticks, tambourines, drums, blocks, bells, and shakers. Have each child play his or her instrument into a tape recorder. Then tape-record the whole group marching around the room playing their instruments at the same time. Let the children listen to themselves playing their separate parts, and then let them hear the whole marching band.

Listening for Pitch

Explain to your children that when you listen for the highness or lowness of a sound, you are listening for pitch. Then gather them in a circle and have them listen as you play notes on a piano, xylophone, flute, or recorder. Invite the children to stretch up high as a tree or a giraffe's neck when they hear high notes and curl up low as a snake, a seed, or a ball when they hear low notes.

Loud and Soft

Teach your children a simple song, such as "Mary Had a Little Lamb," or "Three Blind Mice." Have them sing it first softly, then medium-loudly, then very loudly. How did the different volumes change the song? Which volume did they like best? Then talk about the dynamics of everyday sounds. Have your children come up with examples of sounds that are soft, medium, or loud. Would a mouse's squeak be soft or loud? What about a lion's roar? How would you classify a dripping faucet or a honking car? Accept all logical suggestions and answers.

Extension: Explain that composers indicate *dynamics*, or how loudly or softly music should be played, using words such as *piano* (soft), *mezzo* (medium), and *forte* (loud).

Name Clap

Gather your children in a circle and begin clapping in a slow rhythm. Invite the children to begin clapping with you so that you are all clapping together in the same rhythm. Continue clapping as you go around the circle saying each child's name in rhythm. If you wish, add an extra challenge to this clapping game. While everyone continues to clap, say your name and then call out the name of someone else in the circle. That person will then repeat his or her name and call out the name of someone else. For example, you might say "Mar-tha, Con-rad." Conrad would then say, "Con-rad, Be-ti-na." Betina would repeat her name and then call out to someone else.

Hint: This makes a good icebreaker at the beginning of the year, especially if there are many new children.

Clapping Around

Have your children pay attention and follow your lead as you clap and sing "Go Like This," below. Try clapping in funny places and positions, such as clapping near your ears, clapping over your head, clapping while bending your body like a rag doll, and clapping while twirling around. Invite your children to come up with other fun ways to clap.

Go Like This

Sung to: "If You're Happy and You Know It"

If you're watching and you see me, go like this. (*Clap, clap.*)
If you're watching and you see me, go like this. (*Clap, clap.*)
If you're watching what I do,
Then you try to do it, too.
If you're watching and you see me, go like this. (*Clap, clap.*)

Heather Tekavec

One-Handed Clap

Have your children practice moving just one hand and isolating it from the other hand. Then show them how to hold one hand still while they clap with the other. Repeat with the opposite hand.

Directional Clap

Clap once and direct the child next to you to clap once; direct the flow of clapping so that it continues around the circle, with each child clapping only once. When the last child claps, reverse the clapping order. Now add rules for your group clapping experience. Explain that if you clap once, the flow of the clapping continues in the same direction. If you clap twice, the direction of the clapping reverses. Continue while interest lasts.

Making Shakers

Because shakers are easy to make and play, they are a great way to add music to your circle time. The following are ideas for quick, impromptu shakers to use while singing "All Shook Up."

* **Box Shaker Drum**—Let your children decorate laundry detergent boxes with tempera paint. When the boxes are dry, set out an assortment of bottle caps, pebbles, dried beans, marbles, jacks, or other small items. Let each child select a handful of items to put in his or her box. Help the children glue their boxes securely shut. (You may wish to use a hot glue gun.)

* **Egg Carton Shaker**— Find empty egg cartons with no holes in the top. Place one or two scoops of uncooked rice or dried beans inside each carton and securely seal them closed with tape. Let your children glue on short crepe-paper streamers or colorful paper scraps for decorations.

* **Honey Bear Shakers**—Remove the lid from a clean bear-shaped honey bottle and place dried pasta, un-popped popcorn, or some other dry, loose material in the bottle. (Be sure to select a material that will not leak from the spout when the bottle is held upside down.) Screw the lid on securely, or glue the bottle shut.

* **See-Through Maracas**—Collect plastic single-serving soft-drink bottles with caps. Thoroughly clean the bottles and remove the labels. Set out the bottles, funnels, and an assortment of noise-making materials such as sand, pebbles, beans, and rice. Let your children pour the mate-rials into their bottles and twist the caps on. Then help the children secure the caps with glue or heavy tape, and write their names on their instruments with a permanent marker.

Hint: Remember to supervise the children carefully when working with small materials such as beans and rice.

All Shook Up

Sung to: "Jingle Bells"

Shake, shake, shake.

Shake, shake, shake.

Shake your shaker high.

Shake, shake, shake.

Shake, shake, shake.

Shake it to the sky.

Shake it high.

Shake it low.

Shake it fast or slow.

Shake it all

Around the room,

And everywhere you go!

Jean Warren

Mouse Shakers

Give each of your children a commercial or homemade shaker, such as those mentioned on page 14. Have them pretend they are little mice who squeak by shaking their shakers. Let the children practice their mouse "squeaks." Then tell your children the story of "The Country Mouse and the City Mouse."

After the story, divide the group into Country Mice and City Mice. Explain that if a sight or sound is something that would be found in the country, the Country Mice should shake their shakers. If what you name would be found in the city, the City Mice should do the shaking. Then talk about sights and sounds from the story, with the Mice shaking their shakers at the appropriate times.

Variation: Use this activity to compare opposites, colors, and shapes. For example, you might divide your group into square mice and round mice. Then name square and round objects.

Spring Rain Shower

Give each of your children a shaker. Use the shakers to orchestrate a rain shower. Begin at one end of the circle and invite two children at a time to shake their shakers very softly and slowly. Gradually build until everyone is shaking fast and loud. Reverse this process until only the first two children are shaking softly and slowly. Brainstorm with the children about other instruments you could use to turn your rain shower into a tempest.

Rhythm Time

Give rhythm sticks and woodblocks to some of your children and triangles to others. As you sing "Hickory, Dickory, Dock," have the children with sticks tap out the clock rhythm, and those with triangles strike the hour.

Hickory, Dickory, Dock

Hickory, dickory, dock,

The mouse ran up the clock.

The clock struck one,

And down he did run.

Hickory, dickory, dock.

Traditional

Additional verses: The clock struck two, And down he flew; The clock struck three, And down he did flee; The clock struck four, He ran to the floor; The clock struck five, And he came alive.

Tap Math

Remove all of the face cards from a card deck. Remind your children that the ace equals the number one. Then shuffle the remaining deck. Gather your children in a circle, and give them each two rhythm sticks. Sit in the middle of the circle as the card dealer. Pick a card from the top of the deck and show it to the group. What number is it? Help your children identify the number by counting the number of shapes. Then have the children tap out that number of beats on their sticks. For example, if you pick the three of diamonds you might say, "This card has three diamond shapes. Let's tap three. One, two, three."

Continue while interest lasts. If you wish, let the children take turns being the card dealer.

Hand Harmonies

As you sit in a circle, encourage your children to experiment with using their hands and bodies to produce musical sounds. Here are a few simple hand and body music ideas to teach them.

Hand Clapping – Have your children clap the palms of their hands together in different ways. Try clapping with palms stretched flat and with palms cupped.

Thigh Slapping – Have the children slap their inner and outer thighs with their hands.

Cheek Clapping – Have the children lightly slap their cheeks with their fingers, opening and closing their mouth to make different sounds.

Head Drum – Have the children knock on various parts of their head as a drum.

Tarzan Drum – Have the children beat their chest with their palms or their fists while singing or humming.

Full-Body Slap – Have the children start at their head and work their way down their body, lightly slapping both their front side and their back side with their palms or the pads of their fingers.

Finger Snapping – Teach the children how to put their thumbs and middle fingers together. Have them press them together and then slide them quickly apart to make a snapping sound.

Moneybags – Fill the children's pockets with coins and have them drum their hands against them.

Hand Rub – Have the children rub their hands together at different speeds. (This also generates heat.)

Candy Roll – Show the children how to rub a piece of cellophane or candy wrapper between their hands. (This will produce a nice crinkling sound.)

Partner Jive

Pair off your children. Invite them to face their partner and gently slap their hands together. Show them how to give each other a "high five" by slapping just one hand each together. Then let older partners work together to make up their own musical routines combining partner slapping, high five, and Hand Harmonies techniques.

Group Drum

Make a group drum by stretching a drum-covering material, such as heavy plastic, waxed paper, or cotton fabric, over the top of a wooden or plastic bowl. Hold the covering in place with a large rubber band. Then show your children how to beat the drum with their hands or the pads of their fingers. Make a game of calling out the name of an animal, such as a horse or snail. Pass the drum around the circle, and give each child a turn to drum fast or slow, depending on what they decide is the speed of that animal.

Drum Moves

Bring your Group Drum to the center of your circle. Invite your children to pretend that they are different animals or objects, such as a herd of galloping horses, nuts falling off a tree, raindrops pitter-pattering on a window, slugs oozing across a leaf, or giants thumping up stairs. Beat the drum at different speeds as the children crawl, walk, or run around your circle. If you wish, let the children take turns being the drummer.

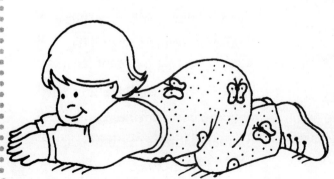

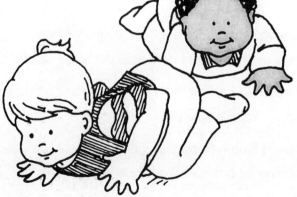

Drumstick Hunt

Drums are not always played by hand. Drumsticks, brushes, or mallets can also be used to produce different drumming sounds. Have your children go on a drumstick hunt throughout your room in search of safe and interesting materials to use as drumsticks. Safe impromptu drumsticks might include wooden dowels, craft sticks, action figures, Lincoln Logs, paintbrushes, thimbles, unsharpened pencils, and measuring spoons. Invite each child to bring one drumstick to the circle. Pass the group drum around your circle and give each child a turn at using what he or she found to drum with.

Hint: Wrap tape or foam around the drumming ends of sticks, pencils, and dowels, to make them safe for both your children and their drums.

Name Chant

Bring a drum to your circle time and set it in front of you. Have each of your children say his or her name aloud. Spend time exploring each name by chanting it several times. Drum the name out on the drum as you chant, and count the number of beats. Accent the main syllable with a stronger drumbeat. Encourage your children to listen and compare the different sounds that names make.

Bell Sounds

Bells can be wonderful props for a circle time warm-up. Give each of your children one or more jingle bells. Have the children act out the motions of the following songs as they sing and ring their bells.

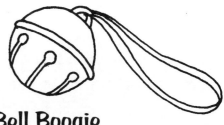

Bell Ringer

Sung to: "Up on the Housetop"

Ring your bell, way up high.

See if you can touch the sky.

Then bend your body down so low.

Ring your bell near your toe.

Ring, ring, ring while you sing.

Twirl, twirl, twirl as you swing and sing.

Ring it fast and ring it slow.

Ring up high and ring down low.

Jean Warren

Bell Boogie

Sung to: "Hokey-Pokey"

You put your bell up,

You put your bell down,

You put your bell in

And you shake it all around.

You do the "Bell Boogie"

And you shake it up and down.

That's what it's all about.

Jean Warren

Jingle Bell Fun

Sung to: "Jingle Bells"

Jingle bells, jingle bells,

Jingle all the way.

Oh, what fun it is to play

My jingle bells today!

Shake them fast,

Shake them slow,

Shake them every way.

Oh, what fun it is to shake

My jingle bells today.

Jean Warren

Bell Stories

Provide each of your children with a bell. Tell your group a simple folk tale, such as the story of "Goldilocks and the Three Bears" or "The Three Billy Goats Gruff." Designate one word, such as *Goldilocks* or *goat*, as a bell-ringing word. Have the children listen carefully for that word and ring their bells whenever they hear you say it.

Variation: Make up a story about bells, such as a sleigh riding story, a church bell story, a fairy story (such as "Peter Pan"), or a Christmas story. Have the children ring their bells as a sound effect every time they hear the word *bell.*

Story Bell

Sit in the middle of your circle with a small bell. Begin a simple story related to the season, an upcoming holiday or event, or a theme that your group has been studying. Ring the bell to invite someone to take your place in the center of the circle and continue your story. Instruct the child in the center to ring the bell when he or she wants to pass the story on to another teller.

Hint: Gently remind each teller before they begin to keep their thoughts short so others can take a turn.

Kazoo Word Play

For each child, cover one end of a paper towel tube with waxed paper, securing the paper in place with a rubber band. Show your children how to hum a tune through the open end of their kazoo. Have them sing or shout fun words into their kazoos, such as *zoom*, *toot*, *moo*, *va-voom*, *la*, *hi*, and *ee-I-ee-I-o*, and feel how the words tickle their lips as they travel through the kazoo. Encourage them also to try singing and saying their favorite words, nursery rhymes, songs, and animal noises into the kazoo.

Megaphone Mania

Show your children how to roll a piece of paper into a cone to make a megaphone. Tape their cones together, if you wish. Divide your circle into two groups and have the two groups stand on opposite sides of your room. Let the two groups shout at each other across the room. Then have them use their megaphones. What happens to their voices?

Using the megaphones, have the two groups sing the "Megaphone Cheer" as an echo/response song, so that each group alternates lines in the song. For example, the first group would sing the first line, then the second group would respond by singing the second line. The first group would sing the third line, while the second group echoes with the fourth line.

Megaphone Cheer
Sung to: "Frère Jacques"

Hear us shouting,

Hear us shouting

Through our megaphones,

Through our megaphones.

We can shout loudly.

We can shout loudly.

Megaphone.

Megaphone.

Additional verses: Hear us whispering, We can whisper softly.

Carol Gnojewski

Cymbal Sounds

Bring to your circle several pot and pan lids that are approximately the same size. Show your children how to hold a lid in each hand by its handle, and clash them together to make thundering cymbal noises. Or have your children brush the lids together, moving one up and one down in a smooth stroke for a less harsh sound. For a different experience, tie string to the handles and show your children how to hold the string in one hand and with the other hand use a stick or brush to strike their lid. Demonstrate how to stop the sound by holding the lid after you hit it. Then play a sequence of hitting or clashing the cymbals together and stopping the sound. Help your children repeat this sequence.

For More Fun: Hold the top of a large baking sheet so that it is in a vertical position, and have your children bang on it with their hands or a wooden mallet. This will make a thunderous sound. In an orchestra, this sound maker would be called a thunder sheet.

Clap-Tap-Clash Music Game

Have everyone practice clapping their hands, tapping their feet, and clashing cymbals together. Show pictures illustrating hands clapping, feet tapping, and cymbals clashing. Place a different number above each picture. Invite your group to make the sounds in the order shown by the pictures. Do the sounds make a tune? Mix up the pictures so the sounds are in a different order. Does the tune sound different?

Sound Symphony

Play several different instruments for your children, or play tapes featuring various instrumental solos. As a group, experiment with using your voices to make the sounds of these instruments. For instance, you might decide a drum makes a rat-tat-tat sound or a rum-pum-pum sound. A guitar might make a strum sound while a horn makes a toot sound. Read the children *Zin! Zin! Zin! a Violin*, written by Lloyd Moss and illustrated by Marjorie Priceman. Invite each of the children to choose which instrument they would like to vocalize as you create a Sound Symphony.

Variation: Explore sounds in tongue twisters and onomatopoetic words, such as *buzz*, *fizz*, *drip*, *plink*, and *splat*.

Vocal Vibrations

Talk about how your voice vibrates when you sing or talk. Explain that all musical sounds are vibrations. Have your children put their hands on their throat and talk or sing to feel this vibration. Do they feel the vibration when they stop talking or singing? If you wish, investigate what vibrates to make sounds when you play other instruments, such as when you hit a drum (the drumhead), when you ring a bell (the hollow cup), or when you play a guitar (the strings).

ABC Warm-up

Warm up your children's mouths and voices by singing "The ABC Song" in your circle. First have the children sing the song very slowly. Invite them to try to pay attention to the way their tongue and lips move as they pronounce each letter. (Holding one hand over your mouth as you sing is a good way to focus attention on all of the facial muscles.) Now have the children try singing the song without moving their mouth. Can they do it? What does it sound like? Next let them move their mouth as much as possible to sing each letter. How does this change the sound?

Group Chant

Have your children sit in a circle. Start them chanting a letter, word, or phrase. As they chant, encourage the children to think about what they are chanting. What does it mean? How does it sound? Do they feel closer as a group as they chant? Then let the children move around while chanting. Have them try to copy each other as they dance and chant. Now have them move and chant freely on their own. How has the experience changed?

Hint: This activity is a good opportunity to introduce new words, foreign language words, or alphabet sounds.

Musical Instruments

Place chairs in a circle facing out. Make sure there is one chair for each of your children. Put a musical instrument on each chair. These can be homemade shakers or bells, or they can be purchased instruments. To start, turn on music from a tape player or radio. Instruct each child to select one instrument and to begin marching around the chairs while playing along with the music. Then turn off the music. Have the children put their instrument on the nearest chair and keep marching. Turn the music back on. When the music resumes, let the children select a different instrument and begin playing again.

Instrumental Movement

Playing an instrument involves the whole body. Show your children pictures of professional musicians playing the instruments included in the song "Let's Play the Instruments." Talk about how the different parts of their bodies are used as they play. As you sing, have the children use movement to suggest what it is like to play these instruments.

Let's Play the Instruments

Sung to: "The Farmer in the Dell"

Oh, let's beat upon our drum,

Let's beat upon our drum

With a *rat-tat-tat*,

And *rat-tat-tat*,

We're playing instruments.

Additional verses: Oh, let's bow our violin, With a *zing-zing-zing*; Oh let's blow our clarinet, With a *toot-toot-toot*; Oh, let's strum upon our harp, With a *plink-plink-plink*.

Steven and Susan Traugh

Instrumental Transition

Use this song to lead your children into circle time.

I Play My Horn

Sung to: "Up on the Housetop"

I play my horn with a *toot, toot, toot.*

Don't you think it's very cute?

I play my drum with a *rum-pum-pum.*

Don't you think it's a happy drum?

Toot, toot, toot, rum-pum-pum.

Toot, toot, toot, rum-pum-pum.

Come with me and join the fun—

I'll play my horn and my happy drum.

Margo S. Hunter

Instrumental Roundup

Begin singing and playing this song to gather your children for circle time. As the children come to your circle, give each a rhythm instrument to play. Have them join in with you until your group has assembled. Adapt the song to the type of instruments the children are using. If there is more than one type of rhythm instrument, add it to the end of the song.

Instrument Sounds

Sung to: "The Mulberry Bush"

This is the sound the little drums make,

Little drums make, little drums make.

This is the sound the little drums make:

Dum ditty, dum ditty, dum.
  (*Bang drums three times.*)

Additional verses: Little bells; shakers; rhythm sticks; instruments. Play three times at end of song.

Dr. Margery Kranyik

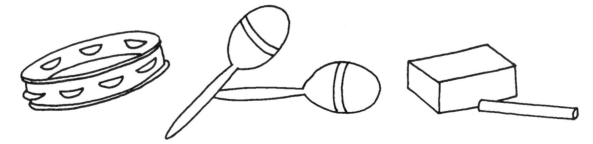

Group Conducting

Explain that a conductor uses a baton to guide the musicians in the orchestra through the music they are playing. Conductors are like storytellers or directors, because they set the tone for playing the music. Give your children dowels, cardboard tubes, or wooden spoons to use as batons. Play a piece of music and let the children sue their batons to "conduct" it.

Conducting Session

Give each of your children a rhythm instrument. Then divide the children into groups or sections determined by the rhythm instrument they are playing. For example, have all of the children with drums sit in one part of the circle while children with bells sit in another. Before you start the music, explain that you are the conductor, and that the children need to pay attention to you as they play. Each section can begin playing only when you point to them with your conducting baton. Then play a familiar song for your children to accompany under your direction. Give the children the opportunity to be conductors, as well.

Classical Music Resources

Check your local library for a variety of classical music. Ask the librarian for specific pieces or additional suggestions. The following selections should get you started.

Quiet pieces: Pachelbel's *Canon in D*; Mozart's *Eine kleine Nachtmusik*, second movement.

Upbeat pieces: Tchaikovsky's *The Nutcracker*; Mozart's *Eine kleine Nachtmusik*, first movement; "In the Hall of the Mountain King" from Grieg's *Peer Gynt*.

Fast pieces: Rimsky-Korsakov's *Flight of the Bumblebee*.

Scary pieces: Mussorgsky's *Night on Bald Mountain*; Prokofiev's *Peter and the Wolf*.

Classical Music

Classical works such as *Peter and the Wolf* by Sergei Prokofiev, *The Nutcracker* by Peter Tchaikovsky, *Hansel and Gretel* by Engelbert Humperdinck, and many others tell stories through music. Over the course of several days, give your children a brief synopsis of the movements of one of these classical selections. Then play the movements for them. See if they can figure out what is happening just by listening carefully. Point out changes in the music and have the children guess what has caused this change. For an extra challenge, see if they can identify which instruments are being used.

Mood Music

In plays, musicals, ballets, operas, films, and television, music is often a device that helps to establish the mood or move the plot along. Play some musical scores or soundtracks for your children. Have them decide if the music is setting a happy mood, a sad mood, a scary mood, or a quiet mood for the story.

Variation: Give the children instruments and have them use them to create a specific mood, tell a story through music, or add sound effects to a spoken story.

Music and Movement

Walking

Gather your children in a circle and talk about walking. What do we use to walk with? How many different ways of walking can your children come up with?

Invite your children to go on a walking tour with you around your circle. Have them listen carefully and follow your directions as you walk together.

Walking Tour

It's time to take a walk. Let's start out with big steps.

Now take even bigger steps.

Now take teeny, tiny steps.

Now try walking on your tiptoes.

Now pretend you're walking up a hill.

Now down a hill.

Now walk sideways.

Now walk backward.

Now bend over and stretch your legs after all of that walking.

Andy Plumb

Footsteps

Prepare several footprint shapes in two colors. Make all the left-foot shapes one color and the right-foot shapes another color. Tape the footprint shapes to the floor in a walking pattern in a circle around your room. Using crepe-paper streamers in the two colors that match the footprints, tape different-colored bands to the ankles of each child. The left bands should match the color of the left footprints, and the right bands should match the color of the right footprints. As the children walk around the circle on the footprints, have them match their bands to the color of the prints. Call out the names of the colors to help them match their gait. For example, if the right-foot color is red and the left-foot color is blue, say, "Red, blue; red, blue," etc.

Hint: This simple movement activity will help reinforce the concept of left and right. Help your children understand that the foot with the red color band is the right foot, and the foot with the blue color band is the left foot. Then call out "right" and "left," instead of "red" and "blue," to match their gait.

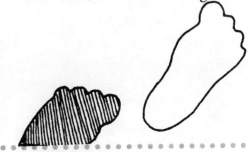

Walk Warm-ups

Use the following rhyming exercises as energy boosters to start the day off on the right foot! These activities also help to reinforce counting skills.

Walk, walk, walk in place.

With a smiley, smiling face.

Stop, rest, and count to ten.

Walk, and walk, and walk again.

Additional verses: Substitute *hop, bend, march,* or *run* for *walk.* Do actions as the rhyme indicates.

Lois E. Putnam

Right on Track

Recite the following rhyme while your children do the movements.

Two steps forward, one step back.

That's good; now you're right on track.

Step one, two. Step three, four.

Now let's try and step some more.

Step five, six, seven, eight, nine, ten.

Let's rest before we step again.

Now we're walking round and round;

Tiptoe and don't make a sound.

Deborah Garmon

Body Walk

Encourage your children to include different parts of their body in their walk, such as their hands, knees, nose, and fingers. Challenge them to walk first on just one body part (hop or crawl), and then work up to walking on three or four body parts.

Extension: Extend this activity into creative drama by helping older preschoolers develop characters to fit their different body walks.

Partner Walk

Pair off your children and have them explore different ways of walking with a partner, such as holding hands, walking back to back, and walking with heads touching. Help the pairs tie together one leg from each child, as if preparing for a three-legged race. Encourage the pairs to work together to make walking in this way seem natural.

Space Walk

Invite your children to pretend they are astronauts walking on the moon. Talk about what an astronaut might wear to take a moon stroll, such as a helmet, a space suit, and space boots. Explain that they need to wear this heavy gear in order to breathe and to keep from floating off into space. Have the children walk about in slow motion. If you wish, spread pillows and cushions on the ground to simulate an uneven moon surface full of hills and craters.

Texture Walk

Define a circle on your floor using materials with different textures, such as masking tape, cotton balls, pillows, sandpaper squares, carpet squares, bubble wrap, plastic garbage bags, or silky fabric. You may want to use tape to fasten these materials to the floor. Ask your children to take off their shoes before they come to your circle. Have them walk on the circle in their bare or stocking feet. How would they describe each material? Which texture did they like the best?

Variation: If you wish, take your circle outside. Use dirt, sand, grass, or bark to make your texture walk.

Paper Trail

Arrange carpet squares on the floor, leaving about 6 inches between each piece. You may want to tape them in place. Have your children line up and follow you as you hop from one square to the next. Lead them to practice hopping forward, backward, and sideways. Have them try hopping on one foot. Let the children take turns being the leader, if desired.

Street Sweepers

Have your children stand with one foot on the ground and one foot raised approximately 3 inches to the side. Instruct them to keep their hands on their hips for balance. Now, have them "sweep" their legs by hopping from one foot to the other. Show them how to slightly bend the supporting leg to protect their knees.

Find a Foot

Find a foot and hop, hop, hop.

When you're tired, stop, stop, stop.

Turn around and count to ten.

Find a foot and hop again.

Find a foot and hop, hop, hop.

When you're tired, stop, stop, stop.

Turn around and count to nine.

Hop, hop, hop—you're doing fine.

Find a foot and hop, hop, hop.

When you're tired, stop, stop, stop.

Turn around and count to eight.

Now let's stop—it's getting late!

Do actions as the song indicates.

Adapted Traditional

Hop One Time

Hop one time,

Hop two.

Hop and hop

Till you are through.

Hop three times,

Hop four.

Hop and hop

And hop some more.

Hop five times,

Hop six.

Do some silly hopping tricks.

Hop seven times,

Hop eight.

Hop a lot.

Now, that's great!

Hop nine times,

Hop ten.

Hop and hop

And hop again.

Lois E. Putnam

Jumping Tricks

Cut candle and stick shapes out of construction paper and tape them, 1 ½ feet apart, to the floor. As you recite "Jumping Children," below, encourage your children to jump over the candle and stick shapes. If you wish, substitute other items for *candles* and *sticks*.

Jumping Children

It's time to jump,
So grab a friend.
First jump over,
Then back again.

Jump over candles,
Jump over sticks.
It's fun to be with friends
And play jumping tricks.

Jean Warren

Learning the Ropes

Bring a jump rope to your circle and lay it out flat on the floor. Invite your children to suggest games to play with the rope. They may want to walk on or along it, or jump over it. Let them try out any safe ideas. Then select a helper to hold one end of the rope while you hold the other. Gently swing the rope back and forth. Have the children jump one at a time, over the moving rope. For an extra challenge, raise the rope higher and higher as the children get better at jumping over the rope. Wiggling the rope is another fun way to vary this activity.

Leaping Lessons

Have your children stand side by side in a line and pretend to be birds or reindeer learning how to fly. Slowly recite "Leap and Fly" below, and have your children follow the movement directions mentioned in the rhyme. Repeat the rhyme, singing a bit faster each time, until the children are leaping and flying through the air.

Leap and Fly

Now we're going to learn to leap,

We'll form a line to begin.

First we'll run and then we'll jump,

Then we'll do it again.

That is how you learn to leap,

Higher every time.

Keep together in the line,

My, we're doing fine!

Now you're going to learn to fly,

It really is quite grand.
  (Stand in open space.)

Just move your arms while you leap,

And watch out how you land.
  (Flap arms while running and jumping.)

Up and up and up you go,

Flying all around.

Careful now—come on back down

And land upon the ground.

Jean Warren

Marching Fun

Set out enough shakers for each of your children in your circle. Sing the following song and let the children march in a circle while shaking their shakers. Pretend that you are a drum major or drill sergeant, and give your children commands as they march, such as "March in place, about face (180-degree turn), half-step (take smaller steps), and double time (take longer, quicker steps)."

Our Kids' Marching Band

Sung to: "Yankee Doodle"

We are marching in a circle,

Shakers in our hands.

Shake them high and shake them low

In our marching band.

Left foot, right foot,

Hup, one, two.

Keep those knees up high.

Left foot, right foot,

Hup, one, two.

Just watch us march on by.

Additional verses: Horns in our hands/Blow them loud and blow them soft; Drums in our hands/Beat them fast and beat them slow.

Susan and Steven Traugh

Marching Together

Sung to: "Skip to My Lou"

Marching together one by one,

Marching together, oh, what fun!
  (*Have children march in a circle.*)

Marching together two by two,

You march with me, I'll march with you.
  (*Have children march in groups of two.*)

Marching together three by three,

Marching together, you can see!
  (*Have children march in groups of three.*)

Marching together four by four,

Marching together, let's march some more.
  (*Have children march in groups of four.*)

Betty Ruth Baker

Pompom Parade

Bands aren't the only groups that march during parades and other festive occasions. Cheerleaders, baton twirlers, and flag-bearing color guards march along with bands and perform routines when the bands stop to play. Provide your children with pompoms or streamers for flags. Have them pretend to be a pompom squad or color guard. Teach them a routine to use their pompoms or flags to marching music. This could be as simple as punching their arms straight out in front of them, lifting them up, and slowly dropping them down. Make sure they spread out so they don't hit each other as they learn the routine. Decide how the group should hold the pompoms or streamers as they march, such as on their hips or in front of their chests. If you wish, have the children march around the room and perform their routine for other groups.

Pompom Cheer

Rah, rah, rah, rah, shout hooray!

The pompom squad is here today.

Thrust out your pompoms
and raise them high;
*(Thrust out pompoms one hand at a time,
and raise them overhead.)*

The pompom squad is marching by.

Carol Gnojewski

Circle Dance

Play some upbeat music and have your children join hands in a circle. Explain that you are going to dance as a group and will need to continue holding hands as you move around. Give your children directions such as these:

- Walk in one direction. Then reverse the direction.
- Skip in one direction. Then reverse the direction.
- Take several steps backward to make the circle as large as it can be.
- Take several steps forward to make the circle as small as it can be.
- Lift hands up. Then all lower hands.
- Move forward as you lift hands up. Move backward as you lower hands.
- All fall down.

Crossover Dancing

Play a varied selection of music, including lively classical, slow classical, jazz, pop, rhythm and blues, country, and rock and roll. Invite your children to form a circle and let the beats and the moods of the music guide their movements as they dance around, maintaining a loose circle. Keep the center of the circle open so that the children can dance from one side of the circle to the other, one person at a time. Invite each child to dance across the circle to change positions at least once.

Color Square Dance

Cut squares out of green, yellow, blue, and red construction paper. Punch a hole in the top of each square. Thread yarn through the holes to make necklaces for your group. Explain that in a square dance, one person is a caller, who calls out the movements that everyone else performs. In a Color Square Dance, the caller instructs dancers to move by color, so the children will need to know the color of their necklace. Have the children form a big circle and dance the "Do-Si-Do" according to the color directions you call out.

Do-Si-Do

Blues step forward

Then turn around.

Walk to your place

And twirl around.

Reds hop to the middle

And back again.

Find the yellows

And shake their hands.

Now greens, you slowly

Turn around.

Clap your hands

And make a sound.

Do-si-do,

Around we go,

All the colors

Step heel to toe.

Jean Warren

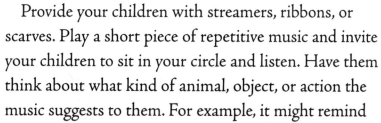

Streamer Dancing

Provide your children with streamers, ribbons, or scarves. Play a short piece of repetitive music and invite your children to sit in your circle and listen. Have them think about what kind of animal, object, or action the music suggests to them. For example, it might remind them of the flight of a bird, the arc of a rainbow, or the twirling of a top. Decide as a group which animal, object, or action you are going to perform as you dance. Begin the music again. Let the children dance with their streamers. As they are dancing, remind them that there is no right or wrong way to suggest the animal, object, or action they have chosen.

Dance Fever

Sung to: "Skip to My Lou"

I like to dance, how about you?
I like to dance, how about you?
I like to dance, how about you?
Please come and dance with me.
Dance, dance, dance, dance, dance.
Dance, dance, I like to dance.
Dance, dance, dance, dance, dance.
Please come and dance with me.

Jean Warren

Have your children stand in a circle. Begin singing the song while your children dance in place. When you get to the line "Please come and dance with me," choose one of the children to come into the middle of the circle and dance with you. Continue until each child who wishes has had a turn dancing with you in the middle of the circle.

Line Dancing

Have your group form a long line. Then explain that a line dance is a type of group dance that is performed in lines. Everyone in each line moves the same way at the same time. As in square dancing, a caller leads everyone through the motions. Play some instrumental country music and teach the children the words and movements to "Here We Go." Alter the movements and words as needed to fit with your choice of music.

Here We Go
Sung to: "Looby Lou"

Here we go up, up, up.
   (Raise hands high.)

Here we go down, down, down.
   (Lower hands and bend down.)

Here we go forward and back.
   (Take a step forward, then back, and clap.)

Here we go round, round, round.
   (Turn around.)

Adapted Traditional

Shadow Dancing

Take your children outside on a warm, sunny afternoon. Have them stand in a circle and look for each other's shadows. Then sing the following song together and have the children watch their magic shadow feet cleverly do everything that they do.

Magic Feet
Sung to: "The Muffin Man"

Have you seen my magic feet,
Dancing down the magic street?
Sometimes fast and sometimes slow,
Sometimes laughing as I go.
Come and dance along with me,
Dance just like my feet you see.
First we'll slide and then we'll hop,
Then we'll spin and then we'll stop.

Do actions as song indicates.

Jean Warren

Be Active

Discuss ways are bodies are active during the day. Then sing the following song and have your children act out the movements. What other types of actions can they think of that involve one part of the body? More than one body part?

Action Words

Sung to: "Twinkle, Twinkle, Little Star"

Blink your eyes
And lick your lips.
Shake your shoulders,
Wiggle your hips.
Kick your leg up.
Wave hello.
Nod your head.
Bend your elbow.
Blink your eyes
And lick your lips.
Shake your shoulders,
Wiggle your hips.

Marie Cecchini

Stand, Swing, and Stretch

Stand in a circle, stoop down low,
Now stand up straight and tall.
Stamp, stamp, stamp your feet,
Now quietly curl up small.
Swing, swing, swing your arms,
Stretch, stretch your spines.
Sway, sway, swing and sway,
Now smile—you're looking fine!

Susan M. Paprocki

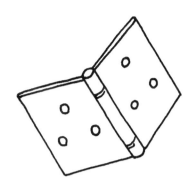

Stiff

Show your children a hinge joint (from a hardware store). Explain that a hinge is designed to enable movement in one direction. Before singing the following song, talk about the joints or hinges we have on our bodies. Where are they located (knees, elbows)?

Extension: Invite your children to pretend they don't have joints. How might they walk, talk, and pick up things without them?

Joint Effort

Sung to: "I'm a Little Teapot"

I can bend my elbows
And my knees.
Then shrug my shoulders
One, two, three.
I can bend my wrists,
My ankles, too.
That's how joints
Help bodies move.

Marie Cecchini

Clap, Clap, Stomp, Stomp

Clap, clap, stomp, stomp, turn around.

Touch your toes; sit on the ground.

Jump up quick, reach for the sky.

You can stretch so very high.

Bend your knees and touch your hair.

Sit down slowly; you're almost there!

Do actions as rhyme indicates.

Janet Reeves

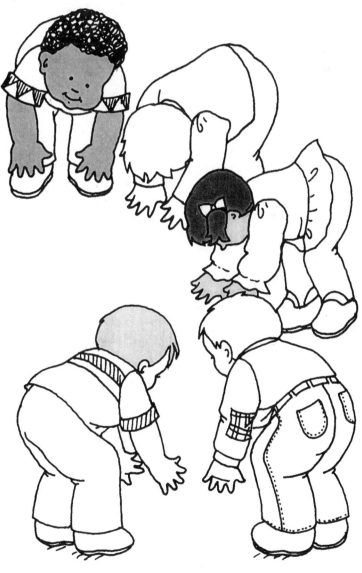

Wiggle Bugs

Sung to: "Yankee Doodle"

Clap your hands and stomp your feet,
Shake yourself around.
Reach your arms high in the air,
Then bend them to the ground.
Nod your head and shake your hips,
Give yourself some hugs.
Lay down flat upon the floor
And pretend you're a wiggle bug!

Do actions as the song indicates.

Diana Nazaruk

I Clap My Hands

I clap my hands, I touch my feet,
I jump up from the ground.
I clap my hands, I touch my feet,
And turn myself around.

I touch my shoulders, then my knees;
I jump up from the ground.
I touch my shoulders, then my knees;
And turn myself around.

I shake my arms and wiggle my hips,
I jump up from the ground.
I shake my arms and wiggle my hips,
And turn myself around.

Do actions as the rhyme indicates.

Adapted Traditional

We Can

We can jump, jump, jump.

We can hop, hop, hop.

We can clap, clap, clap.

We can stomp, stomp, stomp.

We can nod our heads for yes.

We can shake our heads for no.

We can bend our knees for a tiny bit

And sit down slow.

Adapted Traditional

Two Feet Go Tap

Two little feet go tap, tap, tap,
  (Tap feet.)

Two little hands go clap, clap, clap.
  (Clap hands.)

A quick little leap up from my chair.
  (Stand up quickly.)

Two little arms reach high in the air.
  (Stretch arms high.)

Two little feet go jump, jump, jump,
  (Jump.)

Two little fists go thump, thump, thump.
  (Pound fists.)

One little body goes round and round,
  (Twirl around.)

And one little child sits quietly down.
  (Sit down.)

Adapted Traditional

Around and About

Around and about, around and about.

Over and under and in and out.

Run through a field, swim in the sea,

Slide down a hill, climb up a tree.

Do actions as the rhyme indicates.

Adapted Traditional

The Bending Song

Sung to: "Three Blind Mice"

My leg bends.
  (*Bend right leg twice.*)

My leg bends.
  (*Bend left leg twice.*)

So does my arm.
  (*Bend right arm twice.*)

So does my arm.
  (*Bend left arm twice.*)

I bend, I stretch, and I jump really high.
  (*Bend forward, stretch up high, and jump.*)

I turn around, I pretend to fly.
  (*Turn in a circle. Stretch out arms as if flying.*)

I'm glad I bend, oh me, oh my.
  (*Bend at the waist to the right and to the left.*)

I like to bend.
  (*Bend at the waist backward, then forward.*)

Janet Reeves

Touch the Sky

Sung to: "Row, Row, Row Your Boat"

Stretch, stretch, stretch up high.

Touch the sky of blue.

Now crunch down to a tiny ball,

And clap your hands, one, two.

Do actions as the song indicates.

Marie Cecchini

I Move

I move, I walk,

I run, I sit.

I stop to catch

My breath a bit.

I jump, I hop,

I skip, and then

I move, I walk,

I run again!

Lois E. Putnam

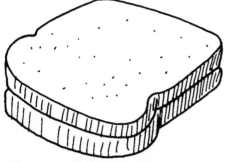

Sandwich Squish

Select one of your children to be peanut butter and one to be jam. Have them stand in the middle of your circle. The rest of the circle is the bread. Together, sing "Hug Sandwich," below, and act out the movements indicated. If you wish, think of other hug sandwiches to make, such as hamburgers, hot dogs, or toasted cheese sandwiches.

Hug Sandwich

Sung to: "I'm a Little Teapot"

I'm the peanut butter.
   (First child points to self.)
I'm the jam.
   (Second child points to self.)
We stick together
When we can.
   (Children in the middle hug each other.)
Bread will gently squeeze us,
   (Circle of children move forward and hug the children in the middle.)
Squish, squish, squish.
We make a yummy
Hug sandwich!

Durby Peterson

Color Code Game

Have your children take a good look at the clothes they are wearing for the day. What colors do they like wearing the best? Adapt the following song to incorporate the colors of your children's clothing. Vary the actions in the last line of the song. If you wish, direct older children to do more than two actions. Make sure to enable every child to participate at least once.

Where Are the Colors?

Sung to: "Oh Where, Oh Where Has My Little Dog Gone?"

Oh where, oh where are the kids with blue on?

Oh where, oh where could they be?

Oh where, oh where are the kids with blue on?

Stand up and twirl around.

Ann-Marie Donovan

Mashed Potatoes

Stand in the middle of the circle and let your children hop all around as you name favorite foods, such as hamburgers, cheese, apples, pizza, salad, celery, and macaroni and cheese. Have them listen for the words "mashed potatoes." When you say, "Mashed potatoes!" it is their cue to drop to the floor and wiggle around. Invite other children to take your place in the middle of the circle and name their favorite foods.

Applesauce!

Explain to the children that the circle is a magic kettle and that you are all apples in the kettle. Together, you are being made into applesauce. Have everyone move to the center of the "kettle" and begin gently bumping into each other, rolling around, and bobbing up and down like apples cooking in a pot. Periodically, call out, "Applesauce!" Whenever you do so, let the children give a huge group hug. Then have the children resume the gentle bumping, rolling, and bobbing.

Following Directions

Collect a carpet square (or use some type of personal mat) for each of your children. Have your children sit on their square, then have them follow simple directions such as "Stand on your square; jump on your square; put one foot on your square; change squares with the person next to you."

Age variation: For older children, you may wish to make the directions more complex. Try giving two- or three-part directions such as "Stand on your square, turn around, and sit down."

Follow the Leader

Stand in front of the circle and invite your children to imitate your actions. Start by clapping, and progress to more difficult actions such as stomping feet, tapping knees, rolling arms, and spinning around. Let the children take turns being the Leader.

Variation: Once the children are familiar with the game, choose one child to be the Guesser. Have the child stand away from the group and turn around with eyes closed. Then choose a new Leader. Have the Leader begin the game, switching activities often. Bring the Guesser back to the middle of the circle. The Guesser has three chances to guess who the Leader is. After three incorrect guesses, the Leader can reveal himself or herself to the Guesser. Let the Leader and the Guesser choose replacements for their roles.

Cattle Call

Have the children pretend to be cows running and grazing around the pasture (your room or your circle). As the farmer, your job is to herd the cows into groups of two to six cows to take them back to the barn. If you pick two, for example, call out, "Two by two." The cows must then scramble to line up in groups of two. Any cows left grazing get to line up with you. Let any child who wants to have a turn as the farmer.

Variation: Change the type of farm animal being herded. Geese, chickens, goats, pigs, sheep, and horses are just a few examples.

Hint: Vary numbers according to group size and counting skill.

Shark Attack

Form a big circle with half of the children in your group. (You may want to have them take a giant step backward so the circle is large.) Invite the children in the circle to pretend to be sharks with big jaw arms. Encourage the rest to pretend to be swimmers. When you say, "Jaws open," the sharks should hold hands and lift them overhead while the swimmers swim freely through the circle. When you say, "Shark attack," the sharks should lower their jaws and run quickly forward, trapping any swimmers left inside. Swimmers caught inside the circle become sharks. Have the groups switch roles periodically.

Pinball

Bring a beach ball to your circle. Have your children sit with their legs spread out in a V shape. Invite them to pretend they are obstacles in a pinball machine. Practice making pinball machine noises such as *whir, buzz, bing, bleep, poing,* and *blam.* Explain that when the ball rolls to a child, he or she can make a pinball-machine noise while batting or kicking the ball away with hands or feet. Continue while interest lasts.

Name Bounce

Stand in the circle with a beach ball or other bouncy ball. Begin the game by bouncing the ball to each child in the circle. After this bouncing and catching practice, call out the name of a child before you bounce the ball. Have that child catch the ball and then bounce it toward someone else in the circle. Remind the children to name the person they are aiming for. Make the game harder by having the children step back to make the circle bigger.

Hot Potato

Hot Potato is a perennial favorite because it's so simple and fun to play. Pass a small ball or beanbag around your circle. Invite your children to pretend it is a real baked potato hot from the oven. They will need to pass it quickly down the circle to avoid burning their fingers. If you wish, play music as the children pass around the "hot potato." When the music stops, find out who is left holding it. That person gets to select the music for the next round.

Hot Potato Variations

- **Theme Potato**—Build upon a current theme your group is studying. For instance, if you are investigating dinosaurs, have the children pass around a small bone or dinosaur toy. If you are learning about squares, pass around a square-shaped item. This activity works especially well for holiday, color, and sensory themes, too.

- **Snack Potato**—Pass around a granola bar or other packaged snack. When the music stops, the child left holding the snack gets to keep it. Repeat with a new snack. Play this a few times before giving a snack to everyone.

- **Surprise Potato**—Pass around a box with a lid. The child left holding the box gets to guess what's inside. Then that child can peek inside and check his or her guess. If the guess is incorrect, he or she can then give the group one hint about the object before the game continues.

- **Adjective Potato**—Pretend that the "potato" is sticky, slimy, cold, sharp, or soft. How does this affect how the children pass it to one another? Think of other words to use in place of *hot*.

- **Cuddly Potato**—Pass around something cuddly, such as a blanket or stuffed animal. The child left holding it gets a group hug.

Over and Under

Arrange the children in your circle so that they are facing the back of the person in front of them. Have them stand in the circle with their legs spread apart. Demonstrate how to bend at the waist and pass a playground ball under themselves, through their legs, to the person behind them. Let the children pass the ball around the circle in this way. Then show them how to pass the ball over their head to the person behind them. As before, continue this movement around the circle. For a final challenge, have the children alternate passing the ball under and over as it moves around the circle.

Juggling

Collect several small balls of different colors. Start your children passing one ball around the circle. Then start a ball going the other way, so that two balls are being passed around the circle simultaneously. See how many different balls your children can pass around in this manner.

Group Weave

Invite two children to stand outside your circle and pretend to be weavers. Give the "weavers" two very long pieces of yarn. Have the children in the circle stand with their arms straight out in front of them and their hands up. Let the "weavers" work together to make patterns as they thread between the yarn in and out between the children in the circle.

Group Sit

Arrange the children in your circle so that they are facing the back of the person in front of them. Invite the children to squeeze together as tightly as they can. Then have everyone sit on the lap of the person in back of them at the count of three. Once you have successfully experienced a group sit, see if your group can move forward while still maintaining a seated position.

Pet Shop

Select one child to be the Pet Shopper. Have that child stand in the middle of the circle. The Shopper must tell the group what type of animal he or she is shopping for. One by one, the children in the circle can pretend to be that animal. Invite each child to move around and make the noise the animal would make. The person in the circle then chooses the animal he wants, and that child becomes the new Pet Shopper.

Tiptoe Chase

Divide the children in your circle into Cats and Dogs. Using tape or chalk, mark one line at one end of your room and a second line at the other. Have the Cats wait behind the first line while the Dogs pretend to be asleep behind the other. Then let the Cats tiptoe silently toward the Dogs. When you say, "Chase!" the Dogs should wake up and chase the Cats. The Cats must then race back behind the Cat line. Any tagged Cats must join the Dogs. Switch roles so the Dogs tiptoe toward the Cats. Continue while interest lasts.

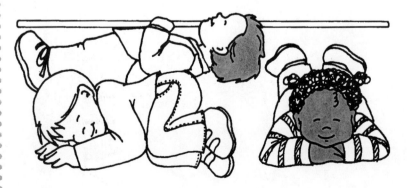

Fish in the Sea

Arrange your children into two rows facing each other. Have the children stick out their arms and hold hands with the person facing them. Recite the poem "Jolly Fishermen" to your children. Ask one child at a time to name a fish or sea creature (be ready to give suggestions). If the child chooses a shark, for example, have that child pretend to be a shark as he or she "swims" under everyone's arms. Incorporate the sea creature the child is pretending to be (a shark) into the second verse of the poem.

Jolly Fishermen

We are jolly fishermen,
Jolly fishermen are we.
Which sea creatures will we see today
As we sail upon the sea?

Shark, shark, shark,
We see a shark.
A shark swam near our boat today
As we sailed upon the sea.

Carol Gnojewski

London Bridge

Arrange your children in two rows facing each other. Have the facing pairs hold their hands together and lift their arms up high to form a bridge. Then have the first pair run under the bridge. When they get to the end of the bridge, have them hold hands and become part of the bridge again. Continue until the children are familiar with the process of running under and re-forming the bridge. Then sing the song "London Bridge." At the end of the first verse, have the children lower their hands, trapping whoever is inside. Then sing the second verse, moving hands from side to side. At the end of the verse, let the children go, and sing the song again. Continue while interest lasts.

London Bridge

London bridge is falling down,
Falling down, falling down.
London bridge is falling down,
My fair lady.

Shake the butter upside down,
Upside down, upside down.
Shake the butter upside down,
My fair lady.

Adapted Traditional

Merry-Go-Round

Divide your children into two groups and form two circles. Arrange the circles so one circle is inside the other. Have the children pretend to be wooden horses or other animals on a carnival merry-go-round. What would their animal look like? How would it move? Play lively calliope music and have the children in both circles move up and down while circling around.

Variation: To make this game more challenging, have the circles rotate in different directions, or add more circles.

Maypole

Cut 8-foot lengths of yarn for each of your children. Loosely tie the yarn lengths around a large Hula Hoop. Stand in the middle of the circle with the Hula Hoop and give each child a yarn end. Pretend that you are a maypole and the children are merry dancers celebrating the first of May. Lift the Hula Hoop over your head and have the children dance around you with their yarn pieces. Let the children take turns being the maypole.

Hint: Depending upon the size of your group, you may need more than one hoop.

No-Lose Duck, Duck, Goose

Tell your children to spread out in a big circle. Then have them take two giant steps backward before they sit down. Select one child to be It. That child will walk around the circle tapping each child lightly on the shoulder and calling out either "duck" or "goose." Remind the children in the circle to listen carefully. If the person who is It calls out "goose," that child must jump up and honk like a goose. It then changes places with the goose, and the game continues.

Variation: Change the name of this game to suit themes or concepts you are working on. For instance, if you are learning about colors, you might call the game Green, Green, Blue. The child tagged as Blue would then point out something blue in the room. If you are studying shapes, you might call it Circle, Circle, Square.

Colored Eggs

Designate one child in your circle to be the Fox while the rest pretend to be Eggs in a basket. Invite the Eggs to decide which color they would like to be. Instruct them not to tell anyone what color they are. Then ask the Fox to name an Egg color. All Eggs of that color must run around the circle and back to their place in the basket before the Fox tags them. Any tagged Eggs become the Fox's helpers. If the Fox fails to tag an Egg, a new Fox is chosen.

Variation: Pass around a basket filled with colored plastic eggs and have each child choose an egg. The color of egg the children choose will determine what color they will be.

Dramatic Play

Group Forest

Show your children pictures of trees. Help them notice the ways branches reach out to the sky. Talk about deciduous trees (trees whose leaves fall off) and evergreens (which stay green year-round). How are these trees shaped differently?

Then make a forest with your children. Invite the children to become trees. Encourage your group to create a mix of deciduous and evergreen trees of varied sizes, shapes, and heights. If you wish, drape colored scarves over the children's "branches" for leaves.

Pick Me

Have your children pretend they are ripe apples on a tree. Would they want to be picked off the tree and cooked into a luscious treat? Or would they rather fall to the ground? What if a worm tried to crawl inside? Talk about all of the wonderful goodies that are made from apples. Then act out the following fingerplay.

Two Red Apples

Sung to: "This Old Man"

Two red apples on the tree.
  (Make two fists and raise them up overhead.)

One for you and one for me.

When I shake, shake, shake the apple tree around,
  (Shake both arms up and down.)

Two red apples come tumbling down.
  (Let your fists drop as the apples come tumbling down.)

Elizabeth McKinnon

Green Garden

Divide your children into two groups, Gardeners and Plants. Have the Plants stay in the circle or a space you have designated as the garden. Then act out the song below, encouraging the Gardeners to sow, water, and weed the garden while the Plants slowly grow from a seed to a flower or vegetable. For a follow-up, help the children sprout some seeds in a flowerpot on a sunny windowsill.

I Will Plant a Garden Green

Sung to: "Old MacDonald Had a Farm"

I will plant a garden green,
Then I'll watch it grow.
I'll dig some holes here in the dirt,
In a nice straight row.
I'll dig one here,
I'll dig one there,
Here a hole, there a hole,
Everywhere a hole, hole.
I will plant a garden green,
Then I'll watch it grow.

I will plant a garden green,
Then I'll watch it grow.
In the hole I'll drop a seed.
Yes, each seed I will sow.
I'll drop one here,
Then I'll drop one there,
Here a seed, there a seed,
Everywhere a seed, seed.
I will plant a garden green,
Then I'll watch it grow.

I will plant a garden green,
Then I'll watch it grow.
I'll water each plant one by one,
They'll sprout up in a row.
I'll water here,
Then I'll water there,
Water here, water there,
Water, water everywhere.
I will plant a garden green,
Then I'll watch it grow.

Steven and Susan Traugh

Picnic Lunch

Bring a basket (a picnic basket if you have one) to your circle. As you pass the basket around the circle, have each of your children pretend to take out an item of food or drink. Have the children hold up the "food" and tell the group what it is. Encourage the children to talk about the size and texture of the food. How might they hold a hot, greasy fried chicken leg differently than a cold, juicy slice of watermelon, a thin peanut butter sandwich, a bunch of grapes, or a large bag of chips? When everyone has some "food," begin to "eat." Have the children think about what it is they are eating as they chew and take bites.

Just Desserts

Have your children pretend to be their favorite desserts. Can they wiggle like gelatin, ooze like frosting, melt like ice cream, or plump up like cinnamon rolls in the oven? Or are they sticky and gooey like caramels or marshmallow treats? Encourage your children to think about how their favorite dessert smells, looks, and feels as it's eaten. Can they think of any other desserts to try to be?

Make It Pop!

Let your group's imaginations make this activity sizzle. Tell the children that they are all popcorn kernels sitting in a hot pan. Have them crouch down low and make sizzling noises. Then have them pretend that they are getting hotter and hotter. What happens when they get really hot? Don't forget the sound effects!

Popcorn Popping

Sung to: "Old MacDonald Had a Farm"

Popcorn popping, oh, what fun,
Popping big and white.
We will wait until it's done,
Then we'll grab a bite.
With a pop, pop here,
And a pop, pop there,
Here a pop, there a pop,
Everywhere a pop, pop.
Popcorn popping, oh, what fun,
Popping big and white.

Elizabeth McKinnon

Pancake Stretches

Talk about pancakes with your children. What do they look and taste like? How are they served? Then have the children spread out on the floor and pretend to be pancakes. Should they lie on their back or on their stomach? If you wish, divide older children into groups of three or more and let them come up with ways to safely stack parts of their bodies, such as hands, arms, and legs, on top of each other. Pretend to pour syrup on the stack and let them wiggle as it spreads all over them.

Earthworms

Bring to your circle a clear-plastic container filled with earthworms. Explain that as earthworms dig their way through the soil, they loosen and soften it, helping the plants to grow. Spread layers of blankets in the middle of your circle and have your children pretend the blankets are soil. Can they wiggle like worms across the floor?

Did You Ever See an Earthworm?

Sung to: "Did You Ever See a Lassie?"

Did you ever see an earthworm,
An earthworm, an earthworm?
Did you ever see an earthworm
Move this way and that?
Move this way and that way
And this way and that way.
Did you ever see an earthworm
Move this way and that?

Betty Silkunas

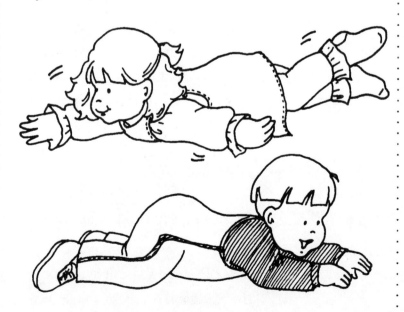

Tunneling

Worms live in the many tunnels they dig in the ground. Talk about what it would be like to live underground. Would you miss the sun? Fresh air? Then have your children form a line. Ask them to spread their legs out wide to form a long tunnel. Pretend that the tunnel ends aboveground. One by one, let each child pretend to be a tunneling worm and crawl through everyone's legs. Invite each child to show you what it might be like to come up out of such a dark place into light.

Variation: Pass a ball down your tunnel instead of crawling through. Have the children use their hands to guide it through their legs.

Ant Scamper

Observing ants and imitating them is always fun for young children. Encourage your children to crawl around on their hands and knees as you recite "Crawly Ant." Then play this movement game. Turn on some music and let them continue crawling and scampering about. Every now and then, turn off the music. Whenever you do so, have them crawl under a table or chair to hide in the "ant nest."

Crawly Ant

I see a little crawly ant
Walk across the floor.
I see a little crawly ant
Walk right out the door.
I see a little crawly ant
Creep out in the sun.
Come again, my crawly ant.
Watching you is fun!

Beverly Qualheim

What's Bugging You?

Explain to your children that when we say something is "bugging" us, we mean that it is bothering us. A lot of people are "bugged" by spiders, bugs, and small animals such as mice and snakes. Have your children pretend that a spider is crawling on their arms, legs, or other body parts. What would they do? How would they get it off? Talk about what to do if you see a spider, bug, or small animal in the room or play yard.

Sticky Web

I just ran into a spider's web,
A sticky, icky spider's web.
It covered my face with silky goo,
But where did the spider go? What should I do?
Now it's on my foot, now it's on my leg.
Now it's on my arm, and it's really big!
Now it's on my nose, and now it's in my hair.
Now I'll set the spider down. It's had a mighty scare.

Carol Gnojewski

Animal Fun

Gather your children in a circle and invite them to become their favorite zoo animals. How do they move about? How would they dance? Have the children pretend that the zookeeper has opened all of the cages. Play some dance music and encourage the children to step outside of their cage (outside of their place in the circle) and find another animal friend to dance with. Then have each animal pair join another pair of animals and dance in a circle. Finally, have all of the zoo animals join together and dance in a big circle.

After a while, stop the music. Now all of the animals are very tired. Have everyone return to their cage (their place in the circle) and sleep as their animals would.

Musical Animals

Ask your children to listen to a few minutes of a piece of classical music. While they listen, have them think about the animal of their choice. Then play the music a second time and let the children pretend to move like their animals. Repeat the activity with different pieces of music.

Black Cat Warm-up

Talk about cats with your children. If you wish, bring in pictures of different cat breeds, or picturebooks with stories and pictures of cats. Then have your children imitate cat movements. Ask them to show how cats walk, play with a ball of string, curl up in front of a warm fire, or drink a bowl of milk. Have them pretend to be cats that are happy, afraid, angry, or hungry.

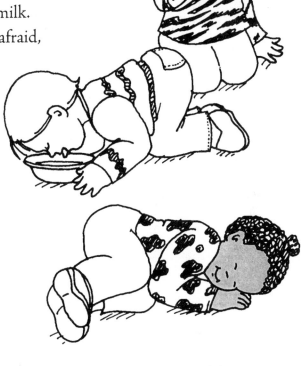

Rocking Horses

Have your children lie on the floor and pretend to be a rocking horse. Show them how to pull their knees as close to their chin as possible. Then invite them to wrap their arms around their legs and "rock" back and forth.

Hint: This stretch is soothing to the muscles in the upper back.

Cobra Stretches

Have your children lie on their stomach with their arms underneath their chest. Their hands should be palms down. Show the children how to use their arms to raise their upper bodies so that they resemble cobras raising their hoods to strike. Make sure that they don't arch their backs too far—this should be a comfortable stretch. Their legs should not move. If you wish, have the children wag their tongue in and out of their mouth like a snake.

Variation: Have one child sit in the middle of the circle and pretend to be a snake charmer while the "cobras" stretch. If you wish, provide the snake charmer with a rhythm instrument to play during the stretching.

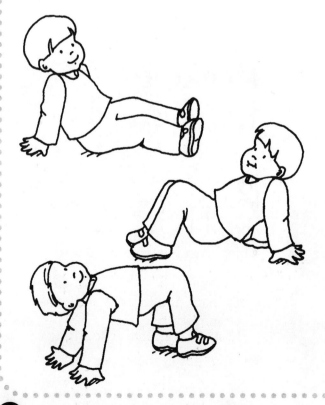

Upside-Down Snake Stretches

Have your children sit on the floor with their legs extended and their arms resting on the floor slightly behind their hips. Next, have them lift their bottom toward the ceiling, keeping their heels on the ground. Invite them to tilt their head back and hold the stretch as long as possible. What other animal might move like this? Why?

Caterpillar to Butterfly

Let your children pretend they are a caterpillar in a cocoon, waiting to become a butterfly. How would it feel to be wrapped up in a cocoon? What might it be like to know that your body is changing and you will wake up as something else? Have each child slowly change into a butterfly and fly around the room meeting other butterflies.

Tadpole to Frog

Designate your circle as a little pond. Encourage your children to pretend they are tadpoles swimming in the water. Have them keep their arms at their sides and their legs together for a tail. Now have them slowly turn into a frog. First grow one hind leg, then grow the other hind leg. Do the same with the front legs (arms). Let the new frogs jump about. How does it feel to have legs to hop on? What is it like to be able to move out of the water onto dry land? Gather all your frogs around the edge of the pond (your circle). Have them sit and croak. Pretend to be a child hunting for pet frogs, and have the children all jump into the pond as you approach.

Animal Walks

Give your children the following instructions during circle time.

Bear Walk

Place your hands on the floor in front of you and take giant bear steps with your hands and feet. Remember to growl like a bear. Keep a nose out for juicy berries.

Bunny Hop

While standing, bend your arms and let your wrists flop in front of your chest. Hop, hop, hop to the carrot patch.

Camel Walk

Place your hands on the floor in front of you and try to keep your legs stiff as you lead the caravan through the desert. Stop at the nearest oasis for a drink of water.

Frog Jump

Squat down, knees facing out, and place your hands on the floor between your knees. Jump up and come back down in this same position. Once you have the technique, hunt for some insects. Remember to "ribbit" and catch insects with your tongue.

Crab Walk

Sit on the floor, place your hands behind you, bend your knees, and keep your feet flat on the floor. Now lift your bottom off the floor. Try to keep your stomach flat. Crabs mostly move sideways, but they can also move forward and backward. Watch out for the crab pots!

Horse Kick

Squat down and place your hands on the floor in front of you. Kick your legs behind you. Try one leg at a time and then both at once. (Be sure to support your weight on your arms and don't kick too high, or you might fall.) Whinny like a horse and watch out for breakable objects or furniture.

The Bunny Hop

Have your children move about the room like bunnies. Then teach your children how to dance the Bunny Hop! Tell them to turn so that they are facing the back of the person in front of them. Have them put their hands on each other's shoulders as if they were linking up to form a choo-choo train. Then have everyone balance on one leg while lifting the other one. Shift balance and lift the opposite leg. Repeat the leg lifts on both sides, and then hop forward three times. Continue these steps as you move around in a circle. If you wish, make up a hopping song to sing as you dance.

Extension: Talk about other animals that hop, such as frogs and kangaroos. How might a dance called the Kangaroo Hop differ from the Bunny Hop?

Hop Like the Animals

Talk with your children about animals that get from one place to another by hopping. Bring in books about these animals to share with your group. Explore what it might be like to hop about all the time. How might you eat breakfast while hopping? Comb your hair?

Weather Kids

Talk about the weather with your children. Look out a window in your room or open the door and have the children describe what is happening with the weather today. Then make your own weather. Perhaps your children would like to become the wind and help the branches twist and bend and keep kites up in the air. Or maybe they would like to be a thunderstorm and light up the sky with lightning or make loud thundering noises. Have them help you make rain fall. Will it be a light sprinkle, a soft, steady rain, or a huge downpour with big wet drops and little balls of hail? Now let them be snowflakes. Have the children think of what they will become once they fall to the ground. Will they cling together in drifts or get rolled into balls and snowpeople? Perhaps some children will come and turn them into snow angels. Or will the sun come out and melt them into pools of water on the ground?

Weather It

Sing the "Weather Song" below and dramatize different types of weather with your children. Have the children think about how they would move if it were rainy, sunny, or snowy. Hold up umbrellas as you walk along singing the first verse. Then fan yourselves and don sunglasses during the second verse. Quickly pull on stocking caps as you shiver and sing the last verse.

Weather Song

Sung to: "Bingo"

There was a time when it was wet

And rainy was the weather.

Rain, rain all around,

Rain, rain all around,

Rain, rain all around,

And rainy was the weather.

Additional verses: There was a time when it was hot, And sunny was the weather; There was a time when it was cold, And snowy was the weather.

Sister Linda Kaman, RSM

Let It Snow!

Let your group's imaginations come into play as you sing "Snowflakes." Place some pillows or soft blankets in the middle of your circle to make snowdrifts. Encourage your children to dance and twirl with you around the circle, pretending to be snowflakes. After the song ends, see how silently everyone can fall to the ground, landing on the snowdrifts.

Snowflakes

Sung to: "Mary Had a Little Lamb"

Snowflakes falling from the sky,
From the sky, from the sky.
Snowflakes falling from the sky
To the earth below.
Watch them as they dance and whirl,
Dance and whirl, dance and whirl.
Watch them as they dance and whirl,
Soft white winter snow.

Judith McNitt

Fog

Explain to your children that fog is a cloud that drifts close to the ground and makes it hard to see. Have your children pretend that they are a mass of fog settling in your circle. Have them roll together around your circle. Some people describe fog as being as thick as pea soup. Talk about other thick things your fog could be like, such as honey, stew, mud, or a monster's breath. Then select two or more children to be a family who have lost each other in the fog. As a group, talk about ways they can break through the fog to find each other again. Perhaps they could call out to each other or use a whistle or horn, such as a foghorn. Or maybe they can signal to each other with flashlights. Have the children act out the scenario they have chosen.

Brighten Your Day

Talk about the sun with your children. What does it feel like? Why are sunny days so much fun? How does it make you feel when you wake up to a sunny day? Then play this sunny game with your children.

Have the children in your circle pretend that there is no sun in their lives. Everything is dark and cold. Ask them to show you their saddest, gloomiest faces. Choose one person to be the Sun. Have the Sun dance around the circle and give everyone a hug. How can they show how happy they are that the Sun has arrived? Invite the children to think of their favorite memories of playing outside in the sun. When the Sun hugs them, have them share these memories by acting them out for your group.

Twister Game

A tornado, or twister, is a destructive, whirling column of air in the shape of a funnel. Talk about what a twister does and show pictures, if possible, of what one looks like. Have any of your children seen one? Explain that the center or eye of a twister is very calm. Then play this no-lose variation of freeze tag with your children.

Draw or form a circle on the floor using chalk or tape. Select one child to be the Twister. The Twister moves all over trying to tag as many people as possible. Anyone tagged by the Twister becomes part of the tornado and must stay inside the circle. Children outside the circle try to retrieve the children in the circle by tagging them before the Twister can catch them. "Eye of the twister" is a control that can be used to make the Twister stay inside the circle and give everyone a rest.

Hint: If you live in an area where tornadoes are common, follow up this game with a discussion about tornado safety. Practice tornado drills with your children. Explain to your children what a tornado siren sounds like, and talk about what to do if they hear one. Make the children aware of everything your facility can do to make them safe during the event of a real tornado.

Feeling Breezy

Give each of your children a scarf. Let them pretend to be the wind and blow all around the room. Ask them to show you soft, gentle breezes; short, strong gusts; and wild, blowing windstorms. What other ways could the wind move? What must it be like to be powerful enough to blow things about? If you wish, have the children pair off. Encourage one partner to be the wind while the other is something blown by the wind. Then have the partners switch roles.

Wind-Chime Circle Game

Bring in wind chimes or a picture of wind chimes, and demonstrate to your children how the wind helps them make music. Then have your children stand in a circle and pretend that they are all chimes being blown by the wind. Take a few minutes to imagine that the wind is blowing. If you wish, play music that suggests the wind or have your children make blowing noises. Encourage them to sway or shuffle together as a unit to simulate the movement of the wind.

Variation: Have your children pretend to be other objects blown by the wind, such as tree branches, flags, tumbleweeds, windsocks, and pinwheels.

Happy Trails

Horse trainers are people who train horses to wear a saddle and obey the commands of the people who ride them. Has anyone in your group ridden a horse? Invite your children to name people who use horses to help them in their work (cowboys, ranchers, farmers, rodeo riders, mounted police officers, carriage drivers, jockeys). Then have the children pretend to be horses while you, as the horse trainer, tell them how to move. (You may want to play some western music to help the children keep their momentum.) First, have the "horses" walk slowly around the circle. Then have them trot or jog a little faster. Next have them lift their legs high and jog a bit faster in a canter. Finally, have them gallop as fast as they can.

Extension: If you wish, bring in a real saddle and bridle for the children to explore.

Race Track

Draw or mark off a circle on your floor with chalk or tape. Tell your children the circle is a race track. Have them pretend to be race cars speeding around the track as they sing "Hop Aboard."

Hop Aboard
Sung to: "Mary Had a Little Lamb"

Hop aboard my little race car,
Little race car, little race car.
Hop aboard my little race car.
Let's drive up and back.
Round and round and round we go,
Round we go, round we go.
Round and round and round we go,
Racing round the track.

Jean Warren

Chug, Chug, Chug

Try playing this movement game with your children. Sing "Little Red Train," pretending to be the engine as you chug around. Each time you sing the song, have someone in your circle hook on behind you as a "car" to make the train grow longer. When the game is over, start a new round and let someone else pretend to be the engine. (If you're playing the game outdoors, you might want to draw chalk railroad tracks on a sidewalk for your train to chug up and down.)

Little Red Train

Sung to: "Row, Row, Row Your Boat"

Here comes the little red train,
Chugging down the track.
It first goes down, then turns around,
Then it chugs right back.
See it hook on cars,
Chugging as it goes.
The little red train never stops,
It just grows and grows!

Jean Warren

Airplane Stretches

Have your children stand with both arms straight out from their sides. Encourage them from pretend their arms are airplane wings. Demonstrate how to rotate their "wings" in a forward motion. Next, have them rotate in a backward motion. Repeat. How might they pretend to be a helicopter, a hot-air balloon, or another type of flying machine?

Hint: This is a good way to energize your children before they "take off" from your circle to engage in other activities.

Balloon Toss

In ballooning you must travel where the wind takes you. A balloon pilot can control only how high a balloon flies and how smoothly it lands—there's no telling where the balloon will land ahead of time!

Have several of your children stand in a circle and pretend that they are air currents helping a hot-air balloon move through the sky. Toss a balloon or beach ball into the circle, and encourage the children to try to keep it up in the air using their hands. Sing the "Floating Balloon" song as you play.

Floating Balloon

Sung to: "Row, Row, Row Your Boat"

Float, float, float the balloon
Gently through the air.
Riding on a river of wind,
How'd it get up there?

Carol Gnojewski

Tour Bus

Taking a ride on a tour bus is a fun way to learn more about a city you are visiting. In these special buses, a tour guide stands at the front of the bus and points out interesting things to see out the window, such as buildings, parks, and statues. Sometimes the tour guide will tell funny stories about the things that you see.

Have your children pretend that they are on a tour bus. Pick one child to be the bus driver, and one to be the tour guide who takes the class on a tour around your room.

Elevator Movement

Talk with your group about elevators and how they carry people to different floors or levels of a building. Then show your children how to move their bodies at different levels. For example, a bottom or first level might be crouching or lying down on the floor. A second or middle level might be bending over at the waist or standing on your knees. A top or third level might be standing on tiptoe or raising your arms to the sky. Once your children are comfortable with these levels, have them pretend they are on an elevator. Call out different levels or floors for them to move to.

Under Construction

Have your children think about all of the construction vehicles they know, such as bulldozers, cranes, and cement mixers. What kinds of things do they do? What kinds of things do they move? Then divide your group into pairs. Invite one person in each pair to pretend to be a construction vehicle while the other person pretends to be something the vehicle needs to move, lift, or mix. Have the pairs switch roles so each person gets to be a vehicle.

Hand Talk

Show your children how to "talk" with their hands. Let them wave hello and goodbye or use their hands to ask someone to stop or be quiet. Show them the "OK" sign. Ask them to think of other things they can say with their hands.

Extension: As a group, make up some hand gestures to use each day. For example, cupping your hands over your ears might be a signal that it's too noisy in the room. Lowering your hands to your lap might be a sign to be still or to keep your hands to yourself.

Talking Hula Hands

Hula dancers use hand movements to act out songs. With your children, make up hand movements for each of these words: rainbow, waterfall, tree, mountain, sea, flowers, bee, dancers, me. Then recite "Over the Rainbow." Let the children use their hand movements to act out the words.

Over the Rainbow

Rainbow over the waterfall,
Rainbow over the tree,
Rainbow over the mountain,
Rainbow over the sea.
Rainbow over the flowers,
Rainbow over the bee,
Rainbow over the dancers,
Rainbow over me!

Jean Warren

Handy Fingerplays

Perform the following fingerplays
with your children.

Hand Washing

One hand,
(Hold out hand.)

Wash another hand.
(Rub hands together.)

Two hands,
(Hold up both hands.)

Wash my face.
(Pretend to scrub face.)

Adapted Traditional

Thank You

My hands say thank you

With a clap, clap, clap.
(Clap hands.)

My feet say thank you

With a tap, tap, tap.
(Tap feet.)

Clap, clap, clap.

Tap, tap, tap.
(Clap hands, then tap feet.)

Turn myself around and bow,

Thank you!
(Turn around, bow, then smile.)

Adapted Traditional

Funny Face

Play a funny-face game with your children. Make different faces for them and see if they can guess how you are pretending to feel. Swap roles and have the children make faces for you. Extend this activity by looking at picture books together. Look at the characters' faces and discuss how they may be feeling.

How I Feel

Sung to: "Twinkle, Twinkle, Little Star"

Sometimes on my face you'll see
How I feel inside of me.
Smile means happy, frown means sad.
When I grit my teeth, I'm mad.
When I'm proud, I beam and glow.
When I'm shy, my head hangs low.

Karen Folk

Farmer in the Dell

Choose one of your children to be the farmer and stand in the middle of the circle. Then sing the song "The Farmer in the Dell." Have the children act out the verses by choosing a partner to stand inside the circle with them.

On the last verse, have the paired children return to the edge of the circle so that the cheese will be left all alone. Talk about what it was like to be chosen or not to be chosen. How did it feel to be left alone as the cheese? This would be a good game to play before talking about feelings.

The Farmer in the Dell

The farmer in the dell,
The farmer in the dell,
Heigh-ho, the derry-o,
The farmer in the dell.

Adapted Traditional

Additional verses: The farmer takes a wife; The wife takes a child; The child takes a dog; The dog takes a cat; The cat takes a rat; The rat takes the cheese; The cheese stands alone.

Emotion Motion

Invite your children to show you how they would move if they were feeling the following emotions:

+ Sad
+ Excited
+ Angry
+ Happy
+ Scared
+ Worried
+ Silly

See if they can show these emotions using their body only, not their face. Think of other emotions to share with your children and have them embody.

Being Mad

Talk with your children about what it feels like to be angry. What do we do when we're angry? How do we show it? How might different parts of our bodies look when we're angry? Let the children show you angry hands, angry necks, angry legs, angry arms, and angry tongues. Before singing "If You're Angry and You Know It," discuss healthy ways of expressing anger and letting it go, such as taking some deep breaths or going to a corner or another room to be alone for a while. Have your children come up with other OK ways to share or release anger.

If You're Angry and You Know It
Sung to: "If You're Happy and You Know It"

If you're angry and you know it, stamp your feet.

If you're angry and you know it, stamp your feet.

If you're angry and you know it,

There are OK ways to show it.

If you're angry and you know it, stamp your feet.

Gayle Bittinger

Additional verses: Take a walk; Count to five; Help a friend.

Job Charades

After singing "Let's Pretend We're Grownups," play a game of job charades with your children. Whisper in one child's ear the name of an occupation such as mail carrier or teacher. Let him or her act out what that person does while the others try to guess what the occupation is.

Let's Pretend We're Grownups

Sung to: "For He's a Jolly Good Fellow"

Let's pretend we're grownups,
Let's pretend we're grownups,
Let's pretend we're grownups,
We'll be anyone we want.

We can drive a fire truck,
We can look after children,
We can work on a farm,
We'll be anyone we want.

Steven and Susan Traugh

Sports Pantomime

Brainstorm with your children to come up with individual and team sports that people participate in as part of a healthy, active lifestyle. Some sports might include basketball, baseball, soccer, rowing, bowling, ice skating, swimming, tennis, jogging, and biking. Let one or two children stand in the middle of the circle and act out the movements of a particular sport. See how long it takes to guess what they are playing.

Things to Be

Invite your children to pretend to be various objects around your room, such as a clock, a door, a window, or a box. How would they move? What would they sound like? If you wish, bring in new items for your children to explore, such as wind-up toys, wooden soldiers, rag dolls, and marionettes. Show the children how these items move. Then have the children imitate them.

Move to the Music

Have your children sit in a circle. Play some rhythmic music such as zydeco, Latino music, African drum music, or other types of ethnic music. Invite the children to become the music and act out what it tells them. Encourage them to use their whole bodies to move with the music. Warm them up by having them do the following:

+ Move their feet to the music.
+ Move just their fingers to the music.
+ Move their head and nothing else.
+ Move their arms and legs only.
+ Move just their stomach. (It may seem silly, but try it!)
+ Move their whole body without standing up.

Partner Fun

Gather your children together and have them pair off. Invite them to work together in the following ways:

+ Pick up a ball and play catch with your partner. Throw it back and forth. The ball is getting bigger and bigger. Now it's so big you can barely catch it. Suddenly it bursts open and lots of little balls roll out onto the floor. Work together to gather all the balls into a large barrel.

+ Pretend your partner is a big piece of white paper. Take out a make-believe paintbrush and paint a picture on the paper.

+ Your partner is a piece of wire. How will you bend him or her?

+ Row a boat with your partner. Lead your partner on a journey around the room.

Body Magnets

Have your children pretend that different parts of their body, such as a finger, an elbow, a knee, or a toe, have become magnets. Let them show you what would happen as they walk by a refrigerator or other object that has a metallic surface.

What's Happening to the Floor?

Invite your children to pretend with you as you lead them on the following fun, guided fantasy.

Beware, something's happening to the floor. It's slippery wet! Oh no, we're sliding all over the place. Our feet are covered with banana peels. Let's take off our shoes and walk in our bare feet. That's better, I think. It must be a very warm day. The floor is getting hotter and hotter. It's covered with red-hot coals! Quick! Everyone hop on tiptoes to keep from burning your feet. Wait a minute. Those aren't hot coals. That's strawberry jam. And someone's spreading peanut butter on top of it. My, it feels so squishy between my toes. Maybe we should try a taste. Yucckkk! Spit it out. That's not peanut butter and jelly. It's turned into quicksand. We're sinking, we're sinking. Help! It's OK, everyone. The floor isn't made of quicksand anymore. Now it's frozen like an ice rink. Well, what are you waiting for? Put on your skates and let's go skating.

Odds and Ends

Use your imagination to think of fun, sensory-filled experiences your children can pantomime for everyone. Make up a different experience for each child in your circle. Here are a few examples to get you started.

- Become a firecracker and start to sizzle and then pop.
- Melt like an ice cream cone.
- Pretend you are a feather falling from the sky.
- Roll like a tumbleweed across the desert.

Slow to Fast

Ask your children to think of things that are slow. Then have them move slow, slower, and slowest. What can they name that is slowest of all? Now have your children think of fast-moving things. Encourage the children to pace themselves so that there is a difference between their fast, faster, and fastest movements. When all of your children are moving their fastest, have them freeze. Ask them to show you what it's like to be absolutely still.

Magic Carpet Ride

Collect a carpet square for each of your children. Arrange the squares in a circle. Have each child sit cross-legged on a square. Invite the children to go on a "magic carpet ride." Let them spread their arms to make "wings," and have them lean one way and then the other. Encourage them to tell what they "see" during their imaginary flight.

Freeze Frame

Invite two of your children to be movie directors while the rest of your group pretend to be film actors. Have Movie Director A pick an action for the group to act out, such as skipping rope, brushing teeth, or raking leaves. (Be ready to give the director suggestions.) Let Director A whisper the action to everyone in the circle. Director B should remain in the middle of the circle with his or her eyes shut. Once everyone knows what to do, Director A should say, "Roll 'em" and Director B should open his or her eyes. That is the actors' cue to begin miming the action. At any time after the action starts, Director A says, "Freeze!" and the actors freeze in position. Director B then has to guess what action the actors were doing. Give Director B three chances to guess before selecting new directors.

Totline® PUBLICATIONS

Teacher Resources

ART SERIES
Ideas for successful art experiences.
Cooperative Art
Special Day Art
Outdoor Art

BEST OF TOTLINE® SERIES
Totline's best ideas.
Best of Totline Newsletter
Best of Totline Bear Hugs
Best of Totline Parent Flyers

BUSY BEES SERIES
Seasonal ideas for twos and threes.
Fall • Winter • Spring • Summer

CELEBRATIONS SERIES
Early learning through celebrations.
Small World Celebrations
Special Day Celebrations
Great Big Holiday Celebrations
Celebrating Likes and Differences

CIRCLE TIME SERIES
Put the spotlight on circle time!
Introducing Concepts at Circle Time
Music and Dramatics at Circle Time
Storytime Ideas for Circle Time

EMPOWERING KIDS SERIES
Positive solutions to behavior issues.
Can-Do Kids
Problem-Solving Kids

EXPLORING SERIES
Versatile, hands-on learning.
Exploring Sand • Exploring Water

FOUR SEASONS
Active learning through the year.
Art • Math • Movement • Science

JUST RIGHT PATTERNS
8-page, reproducible pattern folders.
Valentine's Day • St. Patrick's Day •
Easter • Halloween • Thanksgiving •
Hanukkah • Christmas • Kwanzaa •
Spring • Summer • Autumn •
Winter • Air Transportation • Land
Transportation • Service Vehicles
• Water Transportation • Train
• Desert Life • Farm Life • Forest
Life • Ocean Life • Wetland Life
• Zoo Life • Prehistoric Life

KINDERSTATION SERIES
Learning centers for kindergarten.
Calculation Station
Communication Station
Creation Station
Investigation Station

1•2•3 SERIES
Open-ended learning.
Art • Blocks • Games • Colors •
Puppets • Reading & Writing •
Math • Science • Shapes

1001 SERIES
Super reference books.
1001 Teaching Props
1001 Teaching Tips
1001 Rhymes & Fingerplays

PIGGYBACK® SONG BOOKS
New lyrics sung to favorite tunes!
Piggyback Songs
More Piggyback Songs
Piggyback Songs for Infants
and Toddlers
Holiday Piggyback Songs
Animal Piggyback Songs
Piggyback Songs for School
Piggyback Songs to Sign
Spanish Piggyback Songs
More Piggyback Songs for School

PROJECT BOOK SERIES
Reproducible, cross-curricular project books and project ideas.
Start With Art
Start With Science

REPRODUCIBLE RHYMES
Make-and-take-home books for emergent readers.
Alphabet Rhymes • Object Rhymes

SNACKS SERIES
Nutrition combines with learning.
Super Snacks • Healthy Snacks •
Teaching Snacks • Multicultural Snacks

TERRIFIC TIPS
Handy resources with valuable ideas.
Terrific Tips for Directors
Terrific Tips for Toddler Teachers
Terrific Tips for Preschool Teachers

THEME-A-SAURUS® SERIES
Classroom-tested, instant themes.
Theme-A-Saurus
Theme-A-Saurus II
Toddler Theme-A-Saurus
Alphabet Theme-A-Saurus
Nursery Rhyme Theme-A-Saurus
Storytime Theme-A-Saurus
Multisensory Theme-A-Saurus
Transportation Theme-A-Saurus
Field Trip Theme-A-Saurus

TODDLER RESOURCES
Great for working with 18 mos–3 yrs.
Playtime Props for Toddlers
Toddler Art

Parent Resources

A YEAR OF FUN SERIES
Age-specific books for parenting.
Just for Babies • Just for Ones •
Just for Twos • Just for Threes •
Just for Fours • Just for Fives

LEARN WITH PIGGYBACK® SONGS
Captivating music with age-appropriate themes.
Songs & Games for…
Babies • Toddlers • Threes • Fours
Sing a Song of…
Letters • Animals • Colors • Holidays
• Me • Nature • Numbers

LEARN WITH STICKERS
Beginning workbook and first reader with 100-plus stickers.
Balloons • Birds • Bows • Bugs •
Butterflies • Buttons • Eggs • Flags •
Flowers • Hearts • Leaves • Mittens

MY FIRST COLORING BOOK
White illustrations on black backgrounds—perfect for toddlers!
All About Colors
All About Numbers
Under the Sea
Over and Under
Party Animals
Tops and Bottoms

PLAY AND LEARN
Activities for learning through play.
Blocks • Instruments • Kitchen
Gadgets • Paper • Puppets • Puzzles

RAINY DAY FUN
This activity book for parent-child fun keeps minds active on rainy days!

RHYME & REASON STICKER WORKBOOKS
Sticker fun to boost language development and thinking skills.
Up in Space
All About Weather
At the Zoo
On the Farm
Things That Go
Under the Sea

SEEDS FOR SUCCESS
Ideas to help children develop essential life skills for future success.
Growing Creative Kids
Growing Happy Kids
Growing Responsible Kids
Growing Thinking Kids

THEME CALENDARS
Activities for every day.
Toddler Theme Calendar
Preschool Theme Calendar
Kindergarten Theme Calendar

TIME TO LEARN
Ideas for hands-on learning.
Colors • Letters • Measuring •
Numbers • Science • Shapes •
Matching and Sorting • New Words
• Cutting and Pasting •
Drawing and Writing • Listening •
Taking Care of Myself

Posters
Celebrating Childhood Posters
Reminder Posters

Puppet Pals
Instant puppets!
Children's Favorites • The Three Bears
• Nursery Rhymes • Old MacDonald
• More Nursery Rhymes • Three
Little Pigs • Three Billy Goats Gruff •
Little Red Riding Hood

Manipulatives

CIRCLE PUZZLES
African Adventure Puzzle

LITTLE BUILDER STACKING CARDS
Castle • The Three Little Pigs

Tot-Mobiles
Each set includes four punch-out, easy-to-assemble mobiles.
Animals & Toys
Beginning Concepts
Four Seasons

Start right, start bright!